An Introduction of the
Holy Spirit to Teenagers

LES RENGSTORFF

WESTBOW·
PRESS
A DIVISION OF THOMAS NELSON
& ZONDERVAN

Scriptures taken from the Holy Bible, New International Version®, NIV®. Copyright © 1973, 1978, 1984, 2011 by Biblica, Inc.™ Used by permission of Zondervan. All rights reserved worldwide. www.zondervan.com The "NIV" and "New International Version" are trademarks registered in the United States Patent and Trademark Office by Biblica, Inc.™ All rights reserved.

Scripture quotations taken from the Holy Bible, New Living Translation, copyright 1996, 2004. Used by permission of Tyndale House Publishers, Inc., Wheaton, Illinois 60189. All rights reserved.

WestBow Press books may be ordered through booksellers or by contacting:

WestBow Press
A Division of Thomas Nelson & Zondervan
1663 Liberty Drive
Bloomington, IN 47403
www.westbowpress.com
1 (866) 928-1240

Because of the dynamic nature of the Internet, any web addresses or links contained in this book may have changed since publication and may no longer be valid. The views expressed in this work are solely those of the author and do not necessarily reflect the views of the publisher, and the publisher hereby disclaims any responsibility for them.

Any people depicted in stock imagery provided by Thinkstock are models, and such images are being used for illustrative purposes only. Certain stock imagery © Thinkstock.

ISBN: 978-1-4908-3545-7 (sc)
ISBN: 978-1-4908-3546-4 (e)

Library of Congress Control Number: 2014907821

Printed in the United States of America.

WestBow Press rev. date: 04/29/2014

Dedication

I dedicate this book to the Holy Spirit who inspired me and guided me in writing this study with teenagers in mind.

Contents

Introduction

What a complex world we live in. So many places giving me different thoughts on what is right and what is wrong. So how can I know what IS right and what IS wrong?

Daily I hear all kinds of things that I can do, or eat, or drink that will make me happy? But none of them brings me any lasting happiness! So how can I find true joy in my life?

I hear so much bad and negative things and so little good. How can I keep from getting depressed?

The world seems to keep beating me down. I feel absolutely worthless. What can I do about this feeling, my self-doubt, and how can I turn it around and build confidence in my life?

There seems to be no hope in this world. Where can I find hope for my life?

In this book, the author is dealing with all these feelings: confusion, doubt, anger, feelings of unworthiness, self-doubt, depression. And you will find the answer for all these! I guarantee it.

You will find that I have divided the book into two main parts. In the first part you will learn who the Holy Spirit is. In the second part, you will learn to apply what you have learned about the Holy Spirit to your own life.

With that said, may I now introduce myself...

I AM THE HOLY SPIRIT

Let ME introduce myself. I am the Holy Spirit. Sometimes I'm called the Holy Ghost. Call ME by either name, it's Me. I would like for us to get acquainted.

Who Am I?

I. First of all, I want you to know that **I AM A <u>PERSON</u>**

Here is some Biblical Proof that I am a PERSON.

A. Jesus addressed me as a PERSON.

In John 14:17 Jesus calls ME the "Spirit of Truth."

Now read John 14:16-26 and notice that Jesus addresses ME as a person.

How many times can you count that Jesus uses personal pronouns such as "he" and "him" in referring to ME in these verses? _____

B. The Bible shows many ways in which I can be *treated* like a PERSON.

Read the following Scriptures and write down the way in which I am being *treated as a PERSON*.

1. Acts 5:3 "Then Peter said, 'Ananias, how is it that Satan has so filled your heart that you have lied to the Holy Spirit and have kept for yourself some of the money you received for the land?'" (NIV) _____

2. Acts 5:9 "Peter said to her, 'How could you conspire to test the Spirit of the Lord? Look! The feet of the men who buried your husband are at the door, and they will carry you out also.'" (NIV) _____

3. Acts 7:51 "You stiff-necked people! Your hearts and ears are still uncircumcised. You are just like your ancestors: You always resist the Holy Spirit!" (NIV) _____

4. Acts 4:30 "Stretch out your hand to heal and perform signs and wonders through the name of your holy servant Jesus." (NIV) _____

5. Ephesians 4:30 "And do not grieve the Holy Spirit of God, with whom you were sealed for the day of redemption." (NIV) _____

C. All the distinctive characteristics of personality are ascribed to ME in the Bible.

There are those who think this means that I have hands and feet and eyes and ears and mouth, and so on, but these are not the characteristics of *personality*, but of parts of the *body*.

There are three distinctive characteristics of personality. They are:

- Knowledge
- Feeling or emotion
- Will

Any entity that <u>thinks</u> and <u>feels</u> (has emotions) and <u>will</u> is a person.

All of these three characteristics of personality—knowledge, feeling (emotions) and will—are repeatedly given to ME in in the Old and New Testaments.

1. The **Knowledge** of the Holy Spirit

    We read in 1 Corinthians 2:10, 11, "but God has revealed it to us by His Spirit. The Spirit searches all things, even the deep things of God. For who among men knows the thoughts of a man except the man's spirit within him? In the same way no one knows the thoughts of God except the Spirit of God." (NIV)

    This shows that I have **knowledge.** I am not just an influence that lights up your mind to understand the truth but a Being who Himself knows the truth.

2. The **Will** of the Holy Spirit

    In 1 Corinthians 12:11, we read "All these are the work of one and the same Spirit, and he distributes them to each one, just as he determines." (NIV)

    This shows that I have a **will.** This verse teaches you that I am not a power that you get and use according to your will but a PERSON who does according to His **will.** The difference is extremely important in your getting into the right relationship with Me. It is at this very point that many people who are after power get off track. They are reaching out after and struggling to get possession of some mysterious and mighty power. They think that if they get this power they can use it however they want to. You will never ever get possession of the power you want until you come to recognize that there is **not** some Divine power for you to get hold of, and use in your own way for whatever you wish. Can you imagine what the world would be like if people could get this power and use it in whatever way they wish? WOW! Just imagine how people might use such power if they possessed it.

3. The **mind** of the Holy Spirit

We read in Romans 8:27, "And he who searches our hearts knows the mind of the Spirit, because the Spirit intercedes for God's people in accordance with the will of God." (NIV)

This passage shows that I have a **mind**. The Greek word in the Bible that is translated "mind" **includes the ideas of thought, feeling and purpose.**

So then in this passage we have all the distinctive marks of personality that are given to ME.

Throughout the Bible you will find that I am a real <u>PERSON</u>.

It is of the highest importance that you know ME as a PERSON.

I am a real person, just as Jesus Christ Himself is a real PERSON.

A. Now I want to talk to you about some things that some people believe about ME that are not correct. So, if you hear them, you will know that they are wrong.

1. Some incorrectly think that if I'm a person, then I've got hands and feet and eyes and ears and a mouth, and so on, but these are not characteristics of personality. They are parts of the body.

2. Some think that I am merely some mysterious and fantastic power that they, in their weakness, can somehow get hold of and use. Let me tell you, this kind of thinking about ME is wrong.

3. I am not a substance that fills you like a glass of water can be filled half way, or two-thirds full.

II. The second thing that I want you to know about me is that I am **GOD.**

A. Check the Bible out and you will see that in it I am called God:

1. Read 2 Corinthians 3:17. Let me explain.

When Jesus rose from the dead after being crucified, he became a life-giving Spirit. (1 Corinthians 15:45)

That means He entered into a new form of existence. This doesn't mean that Jesus is now without a body or that he became the Holy Spirit. It means that he entered into a new form of existence when he was glorified. As such, he can live in heaven and in the hearts of believers at the same time. Admittedly, this is a mystery. So the important thing to remember is that when Jesus rose from the dead, he became a life-giving Spirit.

2. In Acts chapter 5 is the account of Ananias and Sapphira selling a piece of land, keeping part of the money for themselves, but bringing the rest to the Apostles as if it were the full amount. Peter, in verse 3, condemns them for lying to the Holy Spirit. Notice that in verse 4 the Holy Spirit is called *"GOD."*

3. Another interesting fact is found in John Chapter 14. Jesus is speaking about the coming of the Holy Spirit into our lives. This passage shows you that the presence of God in your life includes the Father and Son, as well as the Holy Spirit.

   The Holy Spirit—"..and He will give you another Counselor to be with you forever—the Spirit of truth." John 14:16-17 (NIV)

   Jesus Christ—"I will not leave you as orphans; I will come to you." (vs. 18) (NIV)

   The Father—"On that day you will realize that I am in my Father, and you are in me, and I am in you." (vs. 20) (NIV)

4. I (the Holy Spirit) have all the divine attributes of God. Read the following Scriptures and list the attribute mentioned.

   Hebrews 9:14

   _____

   Psalm 139:7

   _____

   Because of this, you can never be lost to the Spirit.

5. Following are some of the Divine things that I do and have done as shown in your Bible.

The divine works of the Holy Spirit are revealed in the following verses of Scripture:

a. I Shared in Creation

Genesis 1:2-3

"In the beginning God created the heavens and the earth. Now the earth was formless and empty, darkness was over the surface of the deep, and the **Spirit of God** was hovering over the waters." (NIV)

b. I Raised Jesus from the Dead

Romans 8:11

"The **Spirit of God**, who raised Jesus from the dead, lives in you. And just as he raised Christ from the dead, he will give life to your mortal body by this same Spirit living within you." (NLT)

c. I Place Believers into Christ's Body

1 Corinthians 12:13

"For we were all baptized by **one Spirit** into one body--whether Jews or Greeks, slave or free--and we were all given the one Spirit to drink." (NIV)

John 3:5:

Jesus answered, "I tell you the truth, no one can enter the kingdom of God unless he is born of water and **the Spirit**." (NIV)

d.   I Proceed from the God the Father

John 15:26:

[Jesus Speaking] "When the Counselor comes, whom I will send to you from the Father, **the Spirit of truth** who goes out from the Father, he will testify about me." (NIV)

e.   I Proceed from Christ

John 16:7:

[Jesus Speaking] "But I tell you the truth: It is for your good that I am going away. Unless I go away, **the Counselor** will not come to you; but if I go, I will send him to you." (NIV)

f.   I Give Divine Gifts

1 Corinthians 12:7-11:

"Now to each one the manifestation of the Spirit is given for the common good. To one there is given through the

Spirit the message of wisdom, to another the message of knowledge by means of the same Spirit, to another faith by the same Spirit, to another gifts of healing by that one Spirit, to another miraculous powers, to another prophecy, to another distinguishing between spirits, to another speaking in different kinds of tongues, and to still another the interpretation of tongues. All these are the work of one and the same Spirit, and he gives them to each one, just as he determines." (NIV)

I am a Person, I am God, and

III. Third, I am a **GENTLEMAN**

I will not force myself into your life. Jesus refers to me as "my peace."

I will prod you.

I will encourage you.

I will try to convict you from Scripture.

But you can stop my work in you by choosing to live without Me. And if you do, I will allow you to live with the result of your choice.

IV. Fourth, you should know that I am **POWERFUL**

A. In this letter to the Colossians, Paul told them that he (Paul) labored for the Lord using all the *energy* which so powerfully worked in him. That powerful energy was ME. (Colossians 1:29)

Read 2 Timothy 1:7. You were not given a spirit of timidity, but a spirit of what? _____

1. I am Powerful enough to raise Christ from the dead.

   Romans 8:11 (write it out here)

   _____

   _____

   _____

2. I am Powerful enough to overcome any problem or circumstance that may come into your life.

   1 John 4:4

   _____

   _____

   _____

3. I am Powerful enough to help you put sin to death and out of your life.

   Romans 8:13

   _____

   _____

   _____

   Romans 8:1 – 2

   _____

   _____

   _____

4. I am Powerful enough to transform you into Christ's likeness.

2 Corinthians 3:18

_____

_____

_____

I am the presence of God in your life.

I am not a substance that fills you like a glass of water can be filled half way or two-thirds full.

A person does not have a little of me and prays for more. I am either living in you or I am not living in you. More than being simply a force or influence, I am a living member of the Trinity (Father, Son, and Holy Spirit) with feelings and a personality.

> The word "Trinity" comes from the Latin noun "trinitas" meaning "three are one." The Trinity expresses the belief that God is one Being made up of three distinct Persons who exists as the Father, Son and Holy Spirit.

V. I am a **GUARANTEE.**

A. I am a Guarantee of Your Inheritance.

Ephesians 1:13 -14

_____

_____

B. I am a Guarantee of What is to Come.

2 Corinthians 5:5

_____

_____

C. I am a Guarantee of Sonship. (See also Galatians 4:4-7)

Romans 8:15

_____

_____

D. I am a Guarantee That We Live in Him.

1 John 4:13

_____

_____

What Kind of Work do I do?

1. I **TESTIFY** OF CHRIST

   John 15:26 (write the verse here)

   _____

   _____

2. I **REVEAL TRUTH**

   John 16:3

   _____

   _____

3. I **CONVICT** PEOPLE

   Read John 16:7 – 11 and write verse 8

   _____

   _____

4. I **CULTIVATE** PEOPLE

   I help people to become more and more like Jesus. The Biblical word
   for this process is *"Sanctification."* (To make holy).

2 Thessalonians 2:13

_____

_____

Galatians 5:22 -23

List the fruit that are cultivated in your life as you are obedient to
my teaching.

_____

_____

_____

_____

Hey! Let's spend a little more time on this Scripture in Galatians.

Galatians 5:22

Do you see what that verse is saying? Do you see the power for you in
this promise?

Wouldn't you like to be able to overcome the peer pressure you get at
school?

Would you like to be able to overcome those temptations that come
into your head that you know are wrong, but that you see all the time
on TV as if it's OK?

Galatians 5:16

What does the Apostle Paul say here that you should do and what is the result if you do it?

_____

_____

Do you see the power in that statement?

Write in your own words. "By living in the Spirit," means that I

_____

_____

You know that you can be led by many many things. What comes to mind that could lead you? _____

Over and over each day you hear these things talking to you.

It is absolutely a must that you choose to listen to and to be led by the Holy Spirit......to be responsive to the Holy Spirit, to let the Holy Spirit take control of your life, and to be guided by the Holy Spirit.

Why, you ask?

The Holy Spirit is the One Who knows the will of God. He was sent to dwell in you to help you do His will, to be all God wants you to be, to be all He designed you to be, and to have all He wants you to have.

WOW! Read that again! What do you think about that???

_____

It's important to remember that the Holy Spirit lives in you and each one of us and He is there to help you. But….you have a choice…remember He's a gentleman…He will not force His will on you. If you choose not to let Him work in your life, then He will not give you what's best for you. So, you see how choosing **not** to be led by the Holy Spirit <u>ties Him up</u> so that He can't accomplish in you what He knows is best for you and what He wants for you. The more you go against His leading, the more you tie Him up and keep Him from working good things in your life. But when you let Him lead you, He accomplishes for you much more than you could ever accomplish on your own. He becomes involved in every decision you make. He leads you with wisdom, and the understanding of God's Word.

Have you ever been with some friends and began feeling uncomfortable inside because you knew what they were suggesting or saying was bad? Remember having that feeling inside you? That kind of uncomfortable feeling may be the Holy Spirit telling you to get out of the conversation or to turn it to something else.

Someone was trying to make a decision as to whether to make an investment with a friend to drill for oil. That evening he prayed about it. First thing the next morning, the thought came to his mind, "There's water in the oil" which made him uncomfortable enough to know that it was a signal not to buy. However, the excitement of making a lot of money, led him to buy in to the drilling project anyway. The drilling took place, the oil was struck, and but there was a lot of water with the oil and it was to such an extent that the well would not be profitable. He bombed out and lost his entire investment! Yes, the Holy Spirit was leading him, but he just wouldn't listen. He wouldn't let Him have control. He tied up the Holy Spirit.

Remember, the Holy Spirit is all wise and He wants the best for you and He knows what's best for you. But you must allow Him control of your life. When the Holy Spirit is leading you, you do not have to understand His leading. You just need to obey the Spirit's leading. Sounds like a "No Lose" situation to me. How about you?

The Work that the Holy Spirit's Presence Accomplishes Within You

Galatians 5:22-23

"But the fruit of the (Holy) Spirit (the work which His presence within accomplishes) is love,

> joy (gladness),
> peace,
> patience (an even temper),
> forbearance),
> kindness,
> goodness (benevolence),
> faithfulness,
> gentleness (meekness, humility),
> self-control (self-restraint." (Amplified Bible)

If you are led and controlled by the Holy Spirit, He will produce this kind of fruit within you! These are character traits that are pleasing to God.

You can't **do** these things, and you can't get them by trying real hard to get them. If you want these traits to grow in your life, you just join your life to His. Jesus said, "Remain in me, and I will remain in you. No branch can bear fruit by itself; it must remain in the vine. Neither can you bear fruit unless you remain in me."

John 15:4

_____

_____

So far we have learned that the work of the Holy Spirit is to:

1. The Holy Spirit **Testifies of Christ** to us
2. The Holy Spirit **Reveals Truth** to us
3. The Holy Spirit **Convicts** us
4. The Holy Spirit **Cultivates** us

_____

In addition to that….

5. I **TEACH** PEOPLE

Read Galatians 5:16-18. Write verse 18 _____

_____

_____

John 14:26 _____

_____

_____

6. I **UNITE** PEOPLE

Read John 17:20-23. What is the effect on the world of seeing that we are one with God and each other?

_____

_____

Unity is so important that Paul implores us to "make every effort to keep the unity of the Spirit." (Ephesians 4:3).

How does Jude describe men who divide the body, and follow their natural instincts? (See Jude 16 – 19)

_____

_____

_____

_____

7. I **STRENGTHEN** & **ENCOURAGE** PEOPLE

Read Acts 9:3 _____

_____

_____

Romans 8:26 _____

_____

_____

8. I **COMFORT** PEOPLE _____

John 14:16 _____

_____

_____

9. I **REFRESH** PEOPLE

Acts 3:19 _____

_____

_____

10. I **GIVE JOY** TO PEOPLE

Luke 10:21 _____

_____

_____

1 Thessalonians 1:6_____

_____

_____

SUMMARY

The Holy Spirit...

1. Testifies of Christ to us
2. Reveals Truth to us
3. Convicts us
4. Cultivates us
5. Teaches us

6. Unites us
7. Strengthens/Encourages
8. Comforts us
9. Refreshes us
10. Gives us Joy

How Do We Become Best Friends?

How Do You Get Me into Your Life?

You receive ME at Baptism.

Please understand that baptism doesn't cleanse you of your sins so that you can later receive ME. God promises to remove your sins in the water of baptism and therefore grant you the gift of His Holy Spirit at that time. It happens at the same time.

Acts 2:38 _____

_____

_____

Forgiveness of sin is coupled with the gift of the Holy Spirit. "**And** you will receive the gift of the Holy Spirit" to live within you.

The Lord commanded the Apostles to wait in Jerusalem until they received the power of the Holy Spirit. This "wait" in Jerusalem applied only to that unusual period in the Apostle's lives between the Ascension of Jesus and His gift of the Holy Spirit at Pentecost. After Pentecost, to wait in connection with the Holy Spirit is never reported. Rather than telling the candidates to "WAIT," Peter offered baptism and the Holy Spirit at the same time.

The Holy Spirit is given along with forgiveness in the act of baptism. Peter doesn't contrast baptism and the gift of the Holy Spirit. He joins them.

There is only one Spirit, and one Baptism. Both come together when one is immersed into Christ for the forgiveness of sin.

Ephesians 4:4-6 _____

_____

_____

Every Christian has ME living within them.

What do you think?

Is it possible to be a Christian and not have ME?

Romans 8:9 _____

_____

Paul tells you in 1 Corinthians 6:15-20 that your body is the temple of the Holy Spirit.

The Bible states that God has given us His Spirit.

Romans 5:5 _____

_____

1 John 3:24 _____

_____

1 John 4:13 _____

_____

What does it mean to be *"filled with the Holy Spirit?"*

We are told to be filled with the Holy Spirit.

    Ephesians 5:18 _____

    _____

- To be filled with the Holy Spirit is to be filled with Christ.

- To be filled with Christ is to be filled with the Holy Spirit.

- God doesn't give you the Holy Spirit just so you may have some uplifting and emotional experiences. God gives you power in order that you may live a victorious Christian life.

- The "filling" of the Holy Spirit not only describes the fact of His indwelling but that you have freely given Him the control of your life.

Give the Holy Spirit control of your **WORDS**.

    Ephesians 4:29 _____

    _____

    _____

Give the Holy Spirit control of your **MIND.**

2 Corinthians 10:5 _____

_____

_____

Give the Holy Spirit control of your **BODY.**

Galatians 2:20 _____

_____

_____

Give the Holy Spirit control of your **EMOTIONS**.

Emotions should not be harbored in your heart that would grieve the Holy Spirit. Sin begins with a thought that evokes an emotion.

Conclusion

HERE ARE SOME THINGS THAT I WANT YOU TO DEFINITELY REMEMBER ABOUT ME:

1. I am the presence of God in your life. I am a living member of the Trinity with feelings and personality.

    The Trinity consists of God, the Father, Jesus, the Son of God, and ME, The Holy Spirit.

2. The Bible describes ME in various ways including:

    I am a person.
    I am God.
    I am a gentleman.
    I am a powerful friend.
    I am a guarantee.

3. You receive me at baptism.

    Every Christian has ME living within them.

4. Being "filled" within ME means not only that you are filled with the presence of God, but that you have welcomed my guidance and control.

5. I am an active part of living a victorious Christian life. Here are some ways that I minister to you:

I Testify to you
I Reveal the truth to you
I Convict you
I Cultivate you
I Teach you
I Lead you
I Unite you and others
I Strengthen and Encourage you
I Comfort you
I Refresh you

There are a lot more things in the Bible about Me, but these are the basics and fundamental things that I want you to understand about me so that we can be the very best of friends.

Tomorrow morning when you wake up, how about acknowledging My presence and say,

"GOOD MORNING, HOLY SPIRIT!"

Developing a Close Relationship

Read the Scripture assigned each day, follow the instruction and develop a deeper relationship with ME and God.

Day 1   **Scripture** John 14:16-26

- What does this passage teach me?

- If I apply this passage to my life, what things should be changed in my life?

- What steps should I plan to take in changing my life to reflect the truth of this Scripture?

- When will I begin taking these steps? Today? This week? What is the first action to take?

- How can I be open to God's guidance and strength in prayer?

Day 2   **Scripture** Jude 16 – 19

- What does this passage teach me?

- If I apply this passage to my life, what things should be changed in my life?

- What steps should I plan to take in changing my life to reflect the truth of this Scripture?

- When will I begin taking these steps? Today? This week? What is the first action to take?

- How can I be open to God's guidance and strength in prayer?

Day 3   **Scripture** Galatians 5:22-23

- What does this passage teach me?

- If I apply this passage to my life, what things should be changed in my life?

- What steps should I plan to take in changing my life to reflect the truth of this Scripture?

- When will I begin taking these steps? Today? This week? What is the first action to take?

- How can I be open to God's guidance and strength in prayer?

Day 4   **Scripture** Romans 8:5-15

- What does this passage teach me?

- If I apply this passage to my life, what things should be changed in my life?

- What steps should I plan to take in changing my life to reflect the truth of this Scripture?

- When will I begin taking these steps? Today? This week? What is the first action to take?

- How can I be open to God's guidance and strength in prayer?

Day 5   **Scripture** Ephesians 2:19-22

- What does this passage teach me?

- If I apply this passage to my life, what things should be changed in my life?

- What steps should I plan to take in changing my life to reflect the truth of this Scripture?

- When will I begin taking these steps? Today? This week? What is the first action to take?

- How can I be open to God's guidance and strength in prayer?

Day 6   **Scripture** Ephesians 3:16-19

- What does this passage teach me?

- If I apply this passage to my life, what things should be changed in my life?

- What steps should I plan to take in changing my life to reflect the truth of this Scripture?

- When will I begin taking these steps? Today? This week? What is the first action to take?

- How can I be open to God's guidance and strength in prayer?

Jerry's Testimony

I (Jerry) grew up in a family who were church goers. About the time I started grade school my home started falling apart with my mom and dad constantly fighting and even becoming violent toward each other. It got so that they were constantly fighting with each other and I was scared and upset at what was happening. So I would go to bed crying with my sister and brother. It was my brother, Tom, who helped raise me when parents seemed to ignore me.

Before I was 10, my mother, sister and I moved to another town where my mother had found work. I didn't want to move and leave my friends, but I had no choice. Well, the rest of my elementary school days, I spent in torment. Being picked on, bullied, called names. I tried to get help from others, but I only found moments of joy in little things that didn't last long. I didn't know it then but I was longing for the joy that Christ would later give me.

In middle school, I became very two faced with my friends. I would tell everybody that I was a Christian (and I believed it), but at the same time I was going down a path that would have led me to suicide, had I not come to Christ. In the 7th grade I was sexually abused and I had to learn to give my problems up to God. I learned that I did not have to handle my problems on my own.

Before graduating from middle school I got into smoking pot and drinking. One day I got caught drinking on the school grounds. I believe that this was God's way of telling me that I needed to get straightened out and get my life back on track. But, I didn't listen to the warning, and fell into a deep depression because of all the troubles that I had and I could see no way out.

The last three months of middle school I switched back over to the school system in the country where I had started and I was happy but inside I was still longing for something but I just couldn't figure out what it was.

At the start of high school, I became friends with more and more Christians who helped me to become a better Christian. However, I still got involved in a few relationships that I should not have. It was at this time that I could no longer say that I am a virgin and cannot give myself wholeheartedly over to the person who will take my hand in marriage one day.

My school holds a church type service every Friday morning and I am starting to get involved there. I found Christ in my life by realizing that I am not fighting all these battles that I have to face alone. Jesus is walking by my side and is helping to keep me on the right track. The Holy Spirit is guiding me and giving me the power to do what is right. There are times where I used to question the existence of God but I have realized it was the devil trying to turn me into his servant instead.

Traci's Testimony

I was raised in a Christian home, but as I got into my teens, I didn't think much about God. God didn't mean much to me. I had all kinds of interests, but God was not one of them. It wasn't until my Freshman year in college that I began feeling the impact of not having a personal relationship with God. I was becoming more and more disillusioned with low self-confidence and where my life was heading. I was searching for some sort of meaning in my life. I had felt this emptiness feeling during my teens, but I'd become very aware of it during this period of my life.

One night as I was researching the supernatural (this included things like ghosts, after-life theories, and telekinesis (I was looking for true meaning of life in all the wrong places), I was suddenly filled with a fearful awareness that I didn't know God, and became worried about my eternal destiny. I started to pray, and prayed for a long time. It was the first time I'd prayed to God in such an intimate and heartfelt way, at least since I was a kid. My prayer was riddled with frustration that life seemed meaningless to me, and desperation to know if God was truly real. I remember repeatedly asking him to show me a sign that he exists. It wasn't a malicious "testing", but a heartfelt desire to be assured that he's really there.

After praying, I felt a sense of relief and got into bed. I started reading. After a short time of reading, I heard a voice say "Traci". It was a soft voice, but it had a firm, direct tone about it. I froze, and cautiously replied, "Yes, God?", as if I instinctively knew it was God. I didn't hear anything else after that though. I was frozen in bed for a while afterwards and couldn't even bring myself to continue reading. I was shocked at the prospect of God revealing himself like that. I kept thinking over and over, "Did God actually just call my name?" It stunned me. I started doing some research online to see if other people had experienced this. I found that many people had.

I also came across the Bible verse, "I have called you by name; you are mine" (Isaiah 43:1), as well as the verse where Jesus says that he calls his own sheep by name and leads them out (John 10:3). These verses really confirmed the experience for me. God had called me. I felt so privileged and grateful that he had graciously answered my prayer in this way. I'd asked for a sign, and he gave me one. This isn't the only way he makes himself known to people though. From what I've read of others' testimonies, he makes himself known in different ways to different people, so I figure he knew that calling my name in an audible way was right for me at the time, especially since I yearned for him to show me that he's real. As it says in the Bible, "If you seek God with all your heart, you will find him" (Jeremiah 29:13).

The experience certainly opened my eyes to His existence and kick-started my interest in Him, but I didn't actually willingly give my life over to him until a few months later. I guess I just had to be led to a place where I was ready to entrust everything to him. I was in a "one foot in and one foot out" situation. When I felt ready to, I joyfully told him that I wanted him to take the reins, forgive me of all the sin in my life, fill me with the Holy Spirit, and make me 'new'. He answered me straight away. I was instantly filled with a burning passion for Him, and my perception started to change dramatically. He was all I could think about, and still is.

For the first time, I had experienced the inner fulfilment and meaning that I'd been so desperate for. It was a real testament of being 'quenched' by the "living water" (the Holy Spirit) that Jesus said he would give to all who turn to him. By no means has everything been totally carefree and easy-going for me since I gave my life to him, because we know that there is on-going spiritual warfare within every believer, but I couldn't imagine my life without God now. Now that my eyes have been opened, a life without God is something I never want to go back to. I'd never been in such a state of joy than when I surrendered my life to him. Knowing Him is worth so much more than anything the world has to offer.

To anyone who isn't sure whether God is real or not - ask him yourself. Talk to Him. He's a conversation away.

"Ask and it will be given to you; seek and you will find; knock and the door will be opened to you" - Jesus (Matthew 7:7)

Ray's Testimony

Ray was employed by a company that was owned by a couple of men who thought only of "What can we do to make more money?" Mattered not whether it was by legal means or non-legal means or who it might hurt.

At one point Ray was asked to sign some documents stating that certain jobs in the company were being completed in accordance with government safety regulations

Ray knew for a fact that they were not. The company had cut corners to save money. Ray refused to sign the false documents.

Ray discussed the situation with the owner of the company and informed him that he could not sign the document because it was an outright lie and the result could jeopardize the safety of many people. (The Holy Spirit was giving Ray that uneasy feeling inside and guiding him to do what was right. Remember, that's one of the things He does.)

The owner asked Ray to come up with how they could fix the situation and how much it would cost the company. As Ray worked on this project and started submitting recommendations, it was obvious that the owner had no intention of altering the way they were doing business.

Ray and his wife started praying about this and what they should do. They asked others to pray for guidance. Should he quit the job? Well, they had just finished building their new house and they had a son in college. What would they do for money? The economy was very bad right then and it would most likely take a long time to get another job and he could not expect a good recommendation from his employer due to the situation.

Ray was led to contact a lawyer to see what he could do. (Think this could be the leading of the Holy Spirit again in Ray's life as he strives to do what's right? That His job isn't it?)

At the lawyer's advice, and after much prayer, Ray continued to refuse to sign the false documents and informed the owner that he was going to inform the government of the safety violations if they would not agree to make the change. Without the change thousands and thousands of people's safety could be at risk.

At this point, the owner got the company's lawyer involved. The two lawyers talked and after some time, an agreement was reached that the company would sign an agreement that they would start making changes to meet the government safety regulations.

At this point the owner was treating Ray as if he was a monster and it became apparent that he could no longer work under these conditions. Again after much prayer and guidance, Ray resigned with separation pay.

Now what? He left a good paying job with no prospects of another job anywhere.

After a short time, Ray was led to an advertisement in the Newspaper about a job which he thought he might be interested in. A completely different job. He called for an interview and within just a few weeks, he had a new job with equal pay and even better benefits and in a Christian atmosphere with well-respected management. The Christmas party at his previous employment had been filled with alcohol and drugs. The Christmas party at his new employment had neither, but was much more enjoyable. Now, that is the Holy Spirit working in one's life!! He promises to work that way in your life if you will let him.

Now the rest of the story....about a year later

Ray's son who had been having difficulty finding a good job in the poor economy saw how much his Dad was enjoying his work, asked his Dad if there was any possibility that he could get a job with the company.

His Dad inquired, but he was told that his son was too young, but since Ray had been doing such a good job for them that they would interview him and if they like him, they would see what they could do about the age restriction.

The interview went well. His Son did well on all the employment exams and now his son is also enjoying his job and making more money that he had dreamed of making and is even training others.

Now that's not some coincidence. That's the Holy Spirit working in a life that gives Him control to do what's right and best! After all, that's his job. We just need to let Him do what He does.

Jim's Testimony

(Note: Writing within a parenthesis is the author's comments)

My name is Jim. Before I was 2 years old my mom and dad had split up. Fortunately, I was loved and cared for unconditionally by both sides of my family. I had an amazing child hood.

When I was around 8 or 9 I figured out how I could get what I wanted, I could play my mom and dad against each other. I started bouncing back and forth from elementary school all the way through high school, playing my mother and father against each other just to get what I wanted. If I didn't get what I wanted here, I would go to the others house and make it sound way worse than my situation actually was. So my parents began to blame each other, when I was the actual problem. I went to church here and there as a kid, but I don't know if I could say I was a follower of Christ. More or less I thought God was real and if I believed that I wouldn't go to Hell.

My dad and I moved to St. Louis where I started high school. Here I met a girl named Sylvia and I thought she was absolutely amazing. She was Godly, lived right, and an amazing Athlete. Just the whole package. She lived for God. And I could tell. She got me going to church and believing in God. But the whole time I wasn't really getting to know God for myself. I knew if I got to know God, she would like me more. So I read about God, but never focused Him as my center point of my life. We dated for a little while and eventually she broke up with me. She completely broke me down. I blamed God for it. Why would He take something from me that made me read the Bible and go to church and act like I was living the right way? I think the key word there is "act". I acted like I knew God when all I really wanted was Sylvia.

At that time I stopped reading the Bible and going to church. And I went back to trying to control everything in my life. My center point from then on was girls, drugs, partying, popularity, the list can go on and on! I would do anything to make sure I got these things. Throughout my life God has given me countless signs that, in my opinion, He was focused on reaching His hand out saying He was the one I wanted. (Now that is the Holy Spirit working in Jim's life, He works to bring people to God). But I had it all figured out, and made excuses every time something happened to me as to why they would happen. Until about a couple of months ago my focus was on girls, drugs, and partying. Before my eyes each one of these things were taken from me one by one.

My senior year of high school I moved back childhood home, and met another girl named Alice.. This girl was also an amazing woman. She cared for people, was a great athlete, and we fell in love. She was not a follower in Christ but a very strong good woman and I pray one day she will accept Christ in her life as I have. I met something else my senior year and that was making money. Having money made me smile more than anything other than Alice at this time. As time passed, Alice realized that I wasn't going very far and all I wanted to do is make money selling drugs for the res of my life. I had no plan. So eventually, she broke up with me.

This was twice as hard as the first girl I had a real relationship with because I couldn't blame God this time, I couldn't blame anyone but myself. I was the reason we broke up. So now I had this huge hole in my heart. The biggest center point in my life was just taken from me. So what in the world do I do to fill that hole? Sell more drugs to make more money and pick up partying even more than I already was. This lasted about 4 or 5 months after Alice and I broke up and God gave me another sign that I chose to let my ignorance and proudness cover up.

The next thing that happened was that while I was out partying.. Someone broke into my Grandmother's house and stole every dime I had and then some. I got back to my Grandmother's house at about 3 in the morning and my grandmother slept through the whole entire thing. Didn't wake up once. Now that I look back on it, that was a sign from God. She could have easily had a heart attack if she was up during the time this took place.

So now, I have no money, no girl to focus on, and no parents that I can play against each other to get what I want. What on earth do I do now to fill this huge hole in my life? I decided to party more and go to more music festivals to sell more drugs to make more money to help me fill this huge hole in my heart that I had. Sounds CRAZY! It's unbelievable how my mind works. I thought that was a good idea somehow. So now this lasted for about a month and half at the most.

A couple of months later my whole entire life would change forever and I will never forget it. I walked into my hallway to go to the kitchen to grab a glass of milk and who did I see storming through my house? About 20 cops. They served me with a search warrant and that was all she wrote. I won't say what all they caught me with but let's just sum it up with plenty of DRUGS. Enough of the right drug to make my bond 150,000 dollars. So in order for me just to get out of jail, it would cost me roughly 15,000 dollars. That was unfathomable for me. I was going to jail and there was not one thing any of my family could do about it.

While I was in jail I sat there, trying to figure out what on earth did I do wrong. What could I have done better? I could not come up with an answer. I picked the Bible up once maybe the first two weeks that I was there, trying to make some sense out of it having been away from it for so long but I was quick to close it. I was blessed by the Lord (again the work of the Holy Spirit) when I got accepted to New Life Lodge Rehabilitation center.. I left jail on a Furlow to go to this rehab center for 28 days. The rehab came and picked me up from jail and took me into their custody for the 28 days. When I got to this rehab center, they asked me if I wanted to do the Faith based program, or the traditional program. Without even thinking twice I said faith based. (That decision is the work of the Holy Spirit guiding Jim toward God)

That might have been the biggest decision I made in my life because little did I know it was going to change my life forever. There was a faith based technician at this rehab. His name was Jeremia. And when I met him for the first time I knew something was different about him. He just glowed to me. He walked and people followed. He talked and people listened. When he introduced himself to me, he said "Hey, the name's Jeremiah. I'm an Alcoholic." WOW, this dude was one that everyone wanted to get to know and you could just tell that he was walking with God and was a recovering alcoholic. I wasn't sure what this recovering Alcoholic had that I so desperately wanted but I was going to find out. (The Holy Spirit will put the right people into your life)

It didn't take him long to figure out I was searching for something desperately, so one day we are sitting in a group session at the rehab and he told all of us to take a sheet of paper out. And to draw two lines down it making three columns in the paper. He told us in the first column, write down what you thought God was as a child. Me personally, as a child, I thought God was this guy that kinda sat on top of the clouds and held this lightning bolt in his hand, waiting for you to mess up so he could smite you or something of that nature! In the second column he told us to write down what we thought God was now. I had no Earthly clue what I thought God was. Or if I even believed there was a God. So all I put in my middle column was a question mark. In the third column, he told us if we could make our God, what would we want him to be. What characteristics would our God have? Me personally, I wanted first of all: A loving God, then I wanted a forgiving, caring and a God that was always there for me. He told us to start praying every single day to this "third column God." So I went to bed that night and started praying not to Jesus or to any God based on any religion. But this "third section God" that was loving, forgiving, caring, and always there for me.

I would say it was my 5th night of prayer to this third section God, and I remember exactly what I prayed. I said, "loving, forgiving, caring, and always there for me God, help me wake up tomorrow morning in a fired up mood and learn something tomorrow". The wake up time at the rehab was 5:30 and I was not a happy camper the mornings previous to this prayer. Well, the next morning after that prayer, I woke up at 5:00 and when I opened my eyes, I could not even think about shutting them! I had more energy then I have ever felt before. I literally shot straight out of bed and screamed at the top of my lungs, "LETS GET FIRED UP THIS MORNING BOYS"! Woke up every single person in my cabin 15 minutes before we had to. This kinda made a few people angry but I honestly couldn't help it--irritated would probably be a better word. Ironically enough, the third day of me waking up fired up in the mornings, everyone in my cabin were having competitions as to who could wake up and get everyone else fired up first! Not only did God answer my simple prayer, he used me to help everyone else wake up in a fired up mood and start the day with smiles on their faces. Isn't that just amazing! (The Holy Spirit answers prayers within you. Good morning, Holy Spirit!)

Well, all I knew was this third section God I prayed to worked. And I wanted more. So I ran back to Jeremiah so interested and wanting more information he could give me about this God. He asked me what my third section God characteristics were so I told him my God was first of all Loving, then forgiving, caring, and always there for me. He opened his Bible and asked me, "You said your God is love, right"? I replied with a big head nod and he turned to 1 Corinthians chapter 13. Paul is pretty much talking about love! It defines what love is. Love is

45

patient, it's not conceited, not boastful, not selfish, and so on. Jeremiah then told me that if my God was love to replace "love" with my God in this chapter. So now my God was not only loving, caring, forgiving, and always there! He was also not boastful, not selfish, not conceited, he didn't act improperly, he didn't weep a record of wrongs, and so forth! This absolutely blew my mind. I dove into the Bible head first! As well as Christian books, really anything that I could get more of this God I really have never known for myself. Every single one of my characteristics of my third section God I made up was in the Bible. This God was loving, caring, forgiving, and always there for me! (The Holy Spirit helps you to understand what the Bible is telling you)

I was reading a book that is called Heaven is For Real, and it's about this 3 and a half year old kid who has a supernatural experience during an appendectomy surgery and he goes to heaven. If you have not read this book I would suggest it to anyone! This book broke me completely down. I remember reading the very last page, my knees trembling, my whole face in tears and at that very moment. I dropped to my knees and I didn't ask God, I begged him to be my savior, I begged him to take over my life I was done living for me. And at that very moment. I literally felt the Holy Spirit enter my body and put a smile on my face that I couldn't wipe away. My jaws literally cramped afterwards. I have never cried and smiled at the same time so hard. It was unbelievable! I was finally done living for me. I gave myself to the Lord. And from then on I was a servant of Jesus Christ. The more I read and prayed the more I felt this indescribable presence of the Holy Spirit.

(The Holy Spirit convicts)

From then on I focused only on one thing as the center point of my life, Jesus Christ! In psalm 8 David says, what is mankind what you are mindful of them, that you care for them! I'm a corrupted partying, sinful, friend of this earth. And you care about me? This hit me home.

I wanted to do everything I had to make this relationship with Jesus even stronger. As time had passed at rehab I was a new man by the end of it. On the 28th day of rehab I went to church in the morning then they took me back to jail. I was super nervous about going back to jail because it's not a very godly place and I was young in my faith and didn't want to take any steps backwards. But I did know one thing, God was with me. When I was put back into my pod at the county jail, there was only one bed open, and surely enough, my bunkie was a mini-nite. Similar beliefs to the Amish. I didn't really know what that meant, and still don't really but all I know is he constantly read the Bible and did not associate with anyone else in the pod.

This was just huge for me, I prayed the next few nights for God to give me the strength to talk to this guy because he was pretty intimidating. He literally didn't talk to one person all he did was read his Bible and pray. Well one day I was talking to people about rehab and how God has changed my life drastically, he popped out of his bed and asked me if I would like to have a Bible study that night. I almost couldn't even say yes I was so shocked. Eventually after an awkward silence from my part I said please that would be awesome! From then on we studied at night and prayed and he shown me so much in the Bible. This guy was so Godly and knew so much I couldn't believe this guy was in jail! He got out a night before I did and I won't go into what his chargers were just know that he was a good man for coming and serving his time. He didn't have to. His charges were from years ago when he was a young kid and he wanted to come back to make it right.

I got out of jail and by the grace of God I'm a new man. I now know what my center point of my life is supposed to be. And the best thing about it is. It can't be taken from me! No one can take my God from me. He is a friend of mine forever now. No girl, no drug, not any amount of money can replace my God. It took a whole lot for me to realize that I'm not in control of my life. It took more than it should. But as human beings I believe we focus so much on these earthly things and why they happen that we miss signs from God constantly. Sometimes we need to stop and listen. God will never lead you wrong or into something you can't handle. And if you believe you can't handle it, know that God is with you. He will make sure you can. If God is for me and you, then who on this earth can stand against us? GOD BLESS!

(Notice how the Holy Spirit was always there urging Jim to make the right decisions. He's a gentleman and did not force Jim to do the right thing; He just kept working with him until Jim did make the decision to follow God. That's how the Holy Spirit works.)

ANSWERS TO PREVIOUS QUESTIONS

I.B Ways the Holy Spirit can be treated like a PERSON. (Pg. 1)

1. He can be lied to.
2. He can be tested.
3. He can be resisted.
4. He can be treated as a healer.
5. He can be grieved.

II.A 4 The Holy Spirit has all the divine attributes of God. (Pg. 2)

Hebrews 9:14 Unblemished (sinless)

Psalm 139:7 Omnipresent (He is present everywhere)

Luke 1:33 The power of God.

IV.A 2 Timothy 1:7 (Pg. 2)

You were not given a spirit of timidity, but a spirit of **power**.

WHAT KIND OF WORK DO I DO?

4. I cultivate people (Pg.)

Paul says we should make up our minds to live in the Spirit and by doing that we will not give in to the temptations and lusts that tempt us to do wrong each and every day.

You can be led by many many things. What comes to mind that could lead you?

Satan, TV, books, magazines, people, your mind, your emotions, your will,

The Holy Spirit

About the Author

When I was growing up in the church, I heard very little about the Holy Spirit. When I did, it was mainly in regards as the Holy Spirit being One of the Trinity.

Even at a bible college, I don't remember being taught much about the Holy Spirit ...unless I was sleeping during that time; nor in graduate school.

I believe the cause of this silence was the reaction by the Christian church to churches that emphasize the Spirit at the neglect of other doctrines. The reaction was to ignore the Holy Spirit and not talk about Him.

It was a year or so after I got out of school that I actually got acquainted with the Holy Spirit and what a difference that made in my life. He added a new excitement and power to my Christian walk.

With this background, the reader can understand why this study is being written. We need to learn more about the presence of the Holy Spirit and His work in our lives. I know, I know, I KNOW that by knowing the Holy Spirit and let him guide your life, the life of any teenager can be one of confidence and joy even though you may be experiencing difficulties.

Les Rengstorff was ordained at the First Christian Church in West Frankfort, Illinois. Attended college at Southern Illinois University, graduated from Milligan College with degrees in Bible and Business Administration. He retired from IBM in 1989 after 30 years of service.

He then joined up with Habitat for Humanity where he volunteered in Americus, Ga. and throughout the middle and eastern U.S.

He has served as a minister at Anchor Christian Church in Bonita Springs, FL, SonRise Christian Church in Naples, FL. and for the past 17 years as Executive Minister at the Naples Christian Church in Naples, FL. During the time, at Naples Christian, he also served as Middle School Youth Leader for several years.